IRELAND

LET'S GET QUIZZICAL

GWION PRYDDERCH

SUMMERSDALE PUBLISHERS LTD
46 WEST STREET
CHICHESTER
WEST SUSSEX
PO19 1RP
UK

WWW.SUMMERSDALE.COM
PRINTED AND BOUND IN CHINA
ISBN: 978-1-84953-595-3

SUBSTANTIAL DISCOUNTS ON BULK QUANTITIES OF SUMMERSDALE BOOKS
ARE AVAILABLE TO CORPORATIONS, PROFESSIONAL ASSOCIATIONS AND OTHER
ORGANISATIONS. FOR DETAILS CONTACT NICKY DOUGLAS BY TELEPHONE:
+44 (0) 1243 756902, FAX: +44 (0) 1243 786300 OR EMAIL: NICKY@SUMMERSDALE.COM

THIS PAIR ONLY APPEARS ONCE
ON THE OPPOSITE PAGE

WHICH ONE OF THE FOLLOWING IS NOT A GENUINE FOLK NAME FOR THE EMERALD ISLE?

A) THE OLD SOD

B) FOUR GREEN FIELDS

C) SHAMROCK ISLAND

DUBLIN

CORK

LIMERICK

GALWAY

WATERFORD

WEXFORD

DUNDALK

SLIGO

ENNIS

TRALEE

KILKENNY

```
A L B D U N D A L K
C I D E F G U H X I
K M J L S M B N H W
I E N N I S L R S E
L R G T U E I S V X
K I A W X E N L Y F
E C L U R L O I C O
N K W I E A A G O R
N W A T E R F O R D
Y G Y D X T C B K A
```

**THE GAELIC PHRASE FOR STOUT IS
LEANN DUBH, WHAT IS THE
LITERAL TRANSLATION?**

A) BLACK BEER

B) MUDDY WATER

C) SWEET DRAUGHT

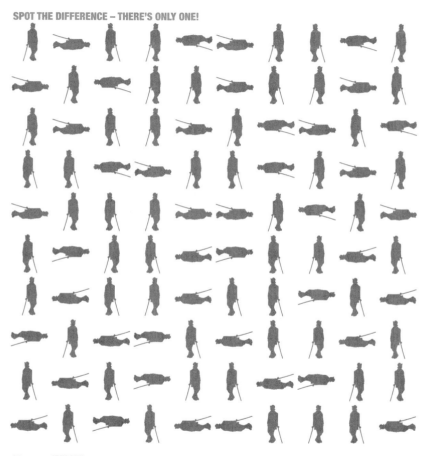

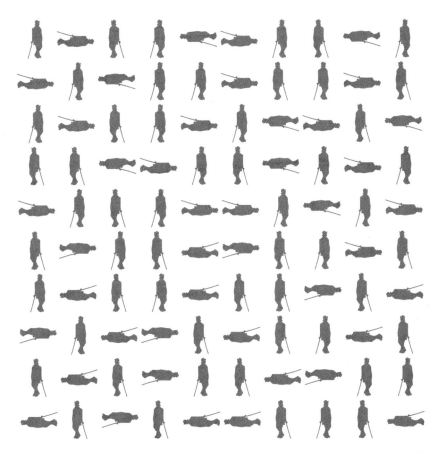

IRELAND IS RENOWNED FOR ITS LOVE OF HORSE RACING, BUT HOW MANY RACECOURSES DOES IT HAVE?

A) 18

B) 26

C) 34

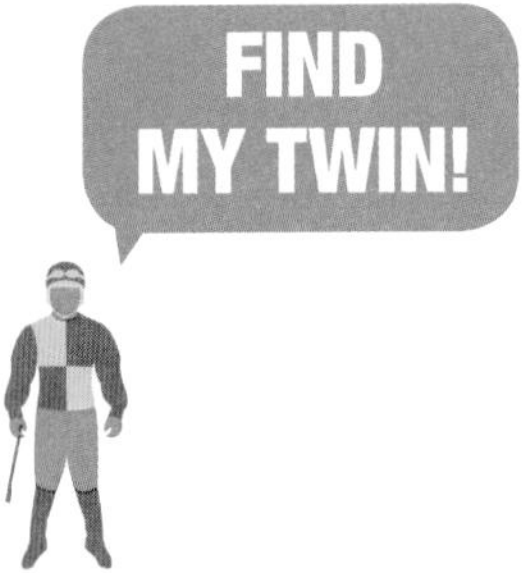
FIND
MY TWIN!

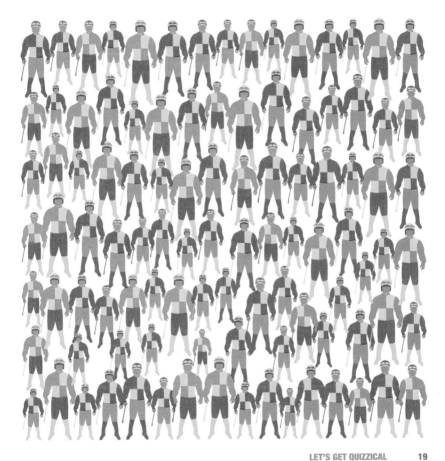

THIS PAIR ONLY APPEARS ONCE ON THE OPPOSITE PAGE

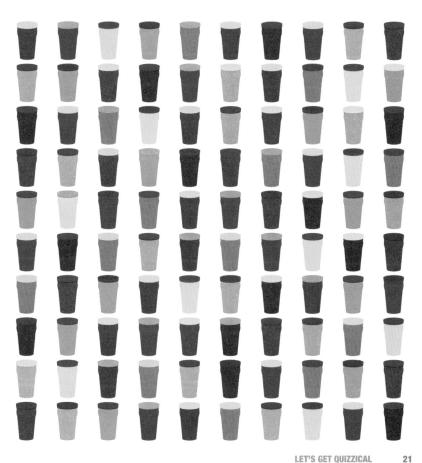

IRISH AUTHOR JAMES JOYCE WAS KNOWN
FOR CREATING NEW WORDS.
CAN YOU GUESS THE MEANING OF
THE WORD 'FADOGRAPH'?

A) A CHART INDICATING POPULAR TRENDS

B) A FADED PHOTO

C) A FAT OLD RAT

**THIS PAIR ONLY APPEARS ONCE
ON THE OPPOSITE PAGE**

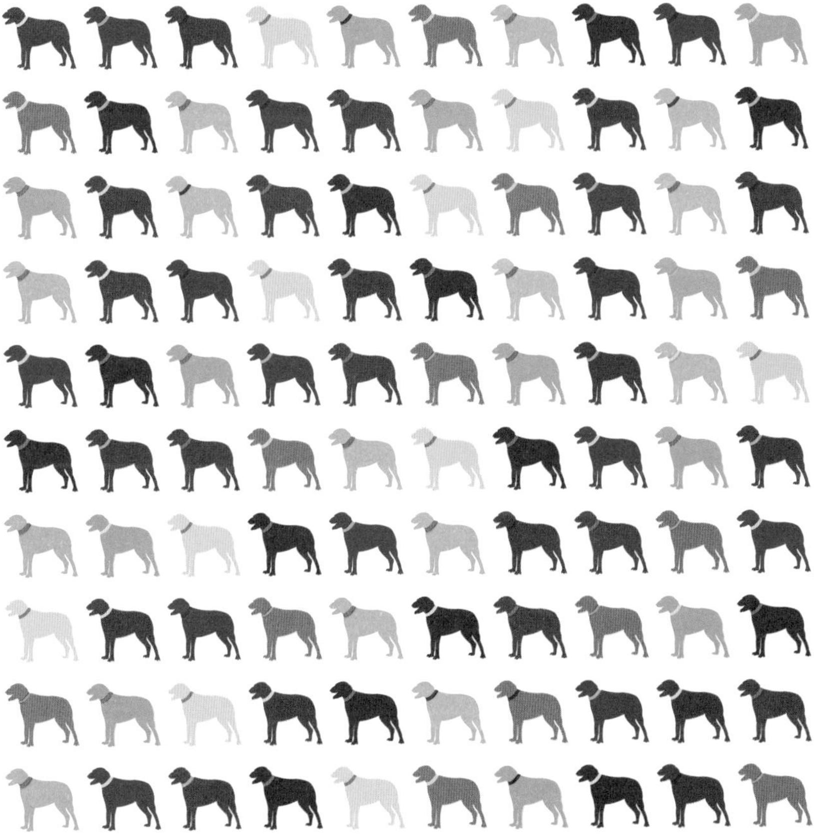

FIND MY POT
OF GOLD!

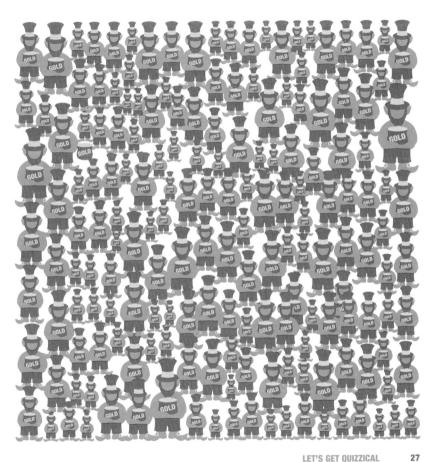

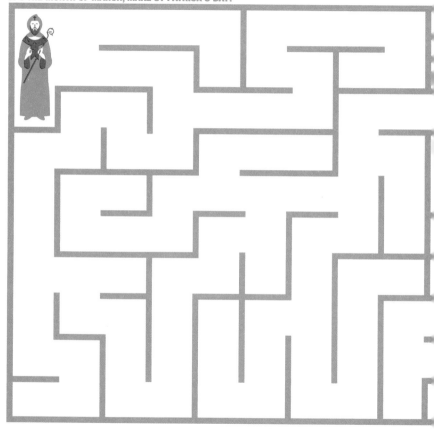

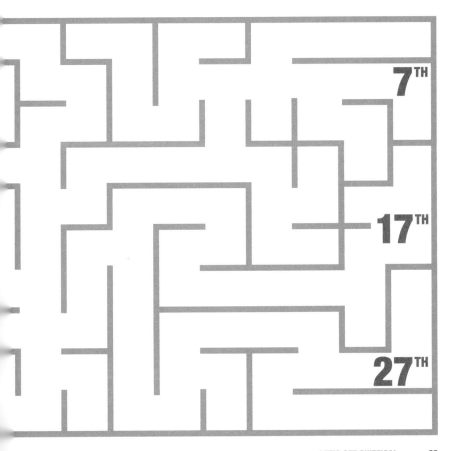

7TH

17TH

27TH

FIND THE 'IRISH PUB'

BLARNEY CASTLE, IN COUNTY CORK, IS HOME TO THE FABLED 'BLARNEY STONE' – BUT WHAT KIND OF STONE IS IT?

A) GRANITE

B) MARBLE

C) BLUESTONE

SPOT THE DIFFERENCE – THERE'S ONLY ONE!

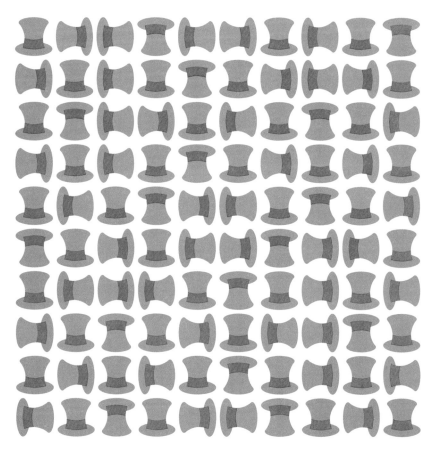

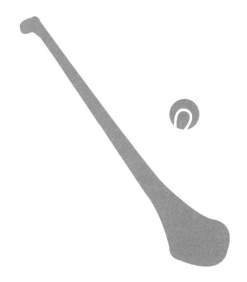

IN THE STICK-AND-BALL GAME KNOWN AS CAMOGIE, THE BALL IS CALLED A...

A) SLIOTAR

B) ROUND

C) BALON

IRISH PUB

IRISH PUB

HOW TALL DOES THE FORMIDABLE IRISH WOLFHOUND (ON AVERAGE, FROM PAW TO SHOULDER) GROW? A MINIMUM OF...

A) 26 IN.

B) 32 IN.

C) 38 IN.

THIS PAIR ONLY APPEARS **ONCE**
ON THE OPPOSITE PAGE

IT'S 9–9 IN YOUR GAELIC FOOTBALL MATCH – GET THAT WINNING GOAL!

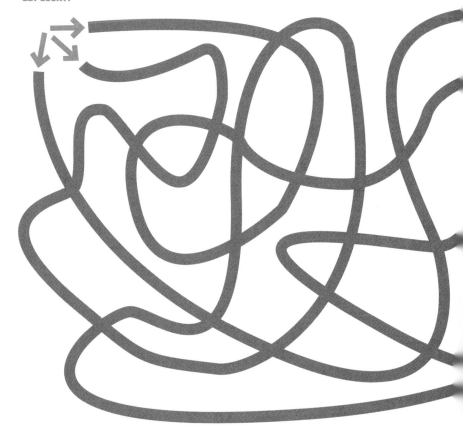

BONO
CORR (ANDREA)
MCFADDEN (BRIAN)
O'DRISCOLL (BRIAN)
O'DONOGHUE (DANNY)
DAY-LEWIS (DANIEL)
FARRELL (COLIN)
O'CONNOR (SINEAD)
KEANE (ROY)
KEATING (RONAN)
BROSNAN (PIERCE)

S	N	K	E	A	T	I	N	G	N
I	L	F	A	R	R	E	L	L	E
W	L	O	D	R	I	N	V	U	D
E	O	F	P	O	A	N	H	K	D
L	C	S	A	N	J	G	R	E	A
Y	S	A	S	F	O	R	M	A	F
A	I	O	S	N	O	B	N	N	C
D	R	P	O	C	N	T	S	E	M
B	D	D	O	C	O	N	N	O	R
C	O	W	E	R	B	T	U	I	O

YOU'RE ODDS-ON FAVOURITE AT KILLARNEY! GO!

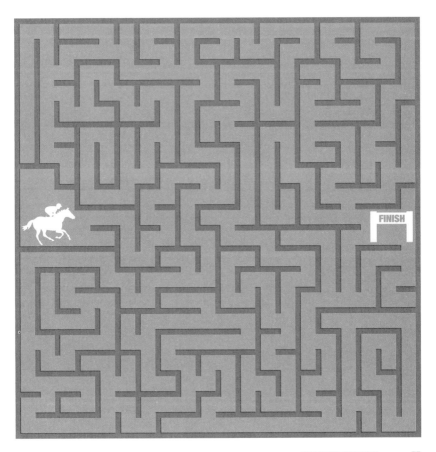

FINISH

WHICH ONE OF THE FOLLOWING FOODS IS A GENUINE IRISH DISH?

A) BODDLE

B) BOXTY

C) BEDA

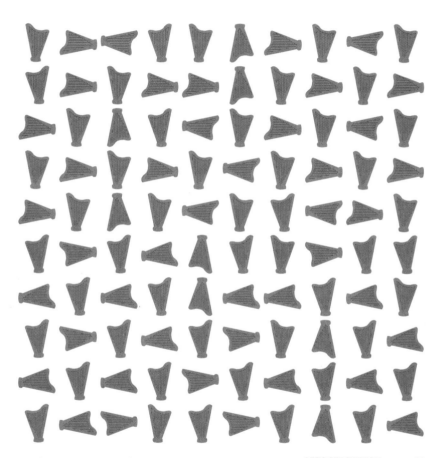

THIS PAIR ONLY APPEARS ONCE ON THE OPPOSITE PAGE

 **FIND THE HORSESHOE!**

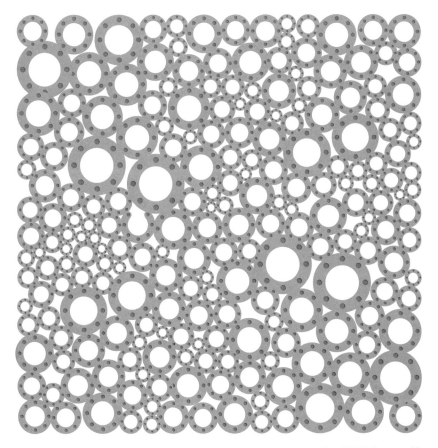

THE SUN'S OUT – BONO NEEDS HIS SHADES!

ACCORDING TO LEGEND, IF YOU CATCH A LEPRECHAUN, WHAT DO YOU RECEIVE IN RETURN FOR HIS RELEASE?

A) HIS POT OF GOLD

B) THREE WISHES

C) ETERNAL YOUTH

 **FIND THE GREEN SHOE**

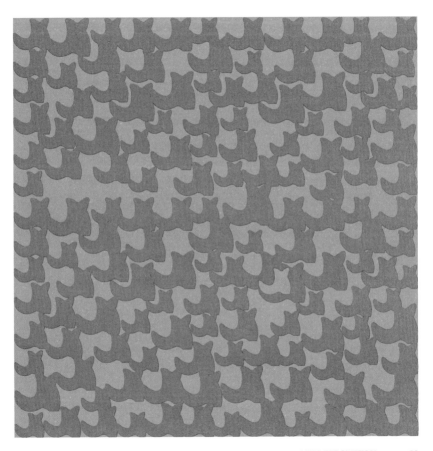

BARMBRACK A BREAD WITH SULTANAS AND RAISINS

BOXTY A POTATO, FLOUR AND BUTTERMILK PANCAKE

CHAMP MASHED POTATOES WITH CHOPPED SCALLIONS

CODDLE BACK BACON WITH SLICED POTATOES AND ONIONS

COLCANNON MASHED POTATOES WITH KALE OR CABBAGE

CRUBEENS BOILED PIGS' FEET

DRISHEEN A TYPE OF BLACK PUDDING

FARL A TRIANGULAR BREAD OR CAKE

GOODY A BREAD PUDDING MADE WITH MILK AND SPICES

GUR CAKE A PASTRY ASSOCIATED WITH DUBLIN

IRISH STEW A LAMB STEW WITH VEGETABLES AND PARSLEY

```
A D B M K X T R L C
I R I S H S T E W O
C I G U R C A K E L
R S X C D O G S L C
U H N C B D H M B A
B E M H R D A S O N
E E F A R L H E X N
E N X M L E X E T O
N S R P G O O D Y N
S B A R M B R A C K
```

WHO, IN THE FOLLOWING LIST, IS NOT AN ALUMNUS OF DUBLIN'S FAMOUS TRINITY COLLEGE?

A) ISAAC NEWTON

B) LORD BYRON

C) SAMUEL BECKETT

**THIS PAIR ONLY APPEARS ONCE
ON THE OPPOSITE PAGE**

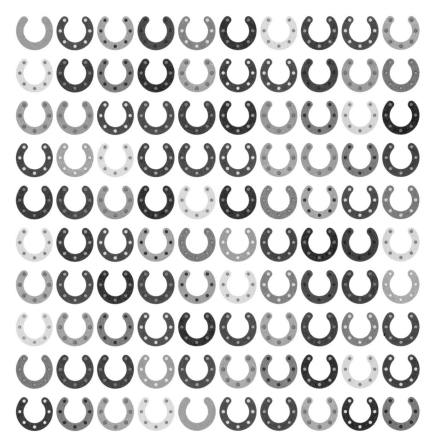

B_____, SLIGO

C_____ OF M_____, BURREN

T_____ S____, LIMERICK

B_____ C_____, CORK

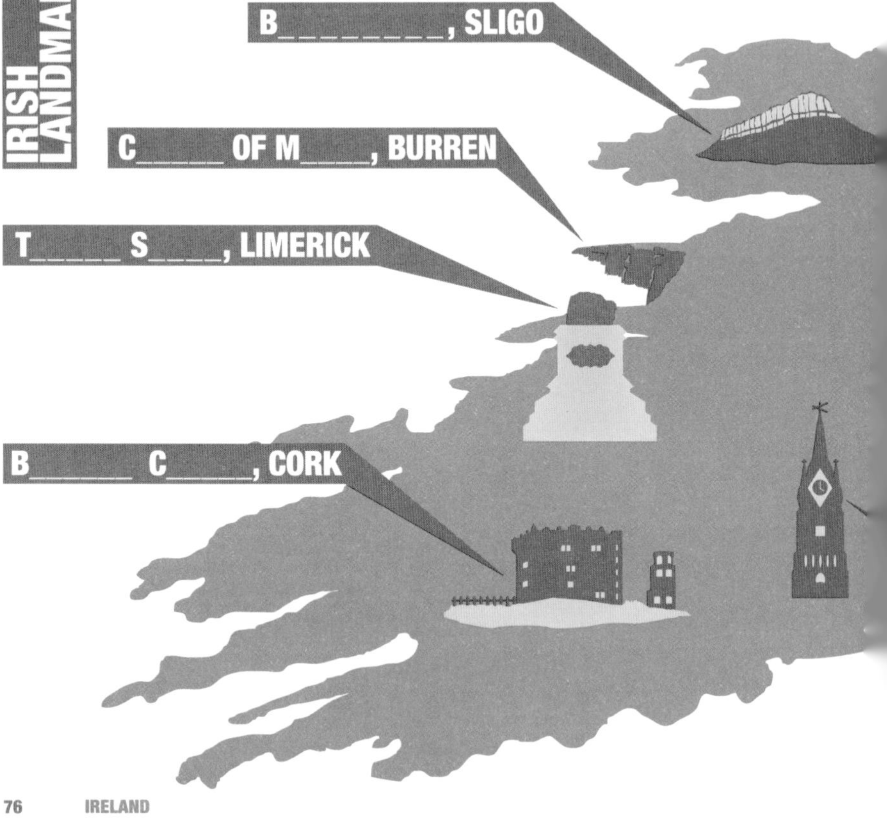

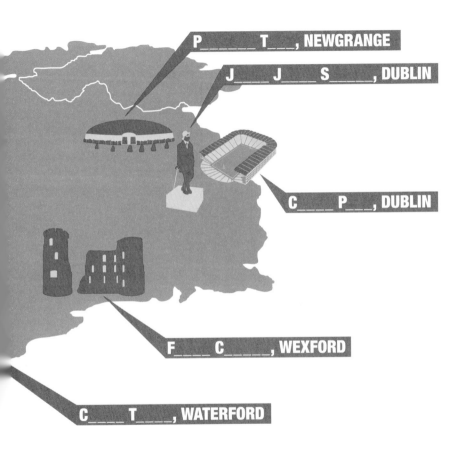

P_____ T___, NEWGRANGE

J___ J____ S_____, DUBLIN

C____ P____, DUBLIN

F____ C_____, WEXFORD

C_ T____, WATERFORD

CÉAD MÍLE FÁILTE

THE PHRASE *CÉAD MÍLE FÁILTE* IS FOUND
ABOVE MANY IRISH PUB DOORWAYS,
BUT WHAT DOES IT MEAN?

A) PEACE BE WITH YOU

B) A HUNDRED THOUSAND WELCOMES

C) EAT, DRINK AND BE MERRY

THIS PAIR ONLY APPEARS **ONCE**
ON THE OPPOSITE PAGE

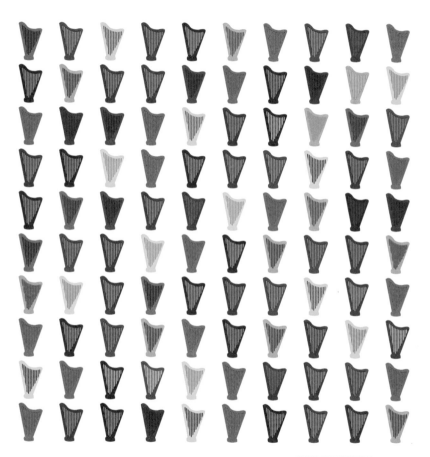

IT'S AD 1169 – GET BACK TO YOUR ROUNDHOUSE, THE NORMANS ARE COMING!

IN THE 1950s IRELAND PRODUCED AN
AMERICAN-STYLE FOUR-SEATER COUPÉ CAR
WITH A CURIOUS NAME – WHAT WAS IT?

A) THE HARP

B) THE SHAMROCK

C) THE BLARNEY

FIND THE ORANGE CLOVER

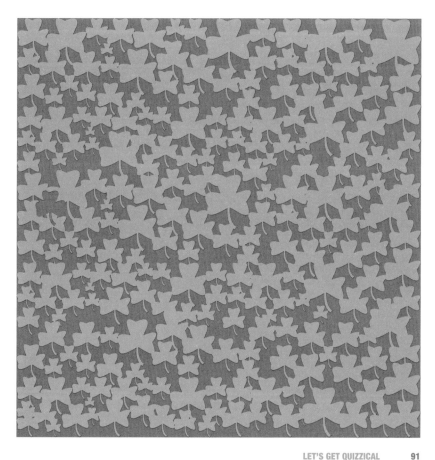

**THIS PAIR ONLY APPEARS ONCE
ON THE OPPOSITE PAGE**

PUT THE CELTIC CROSS BACK TOGETHER!

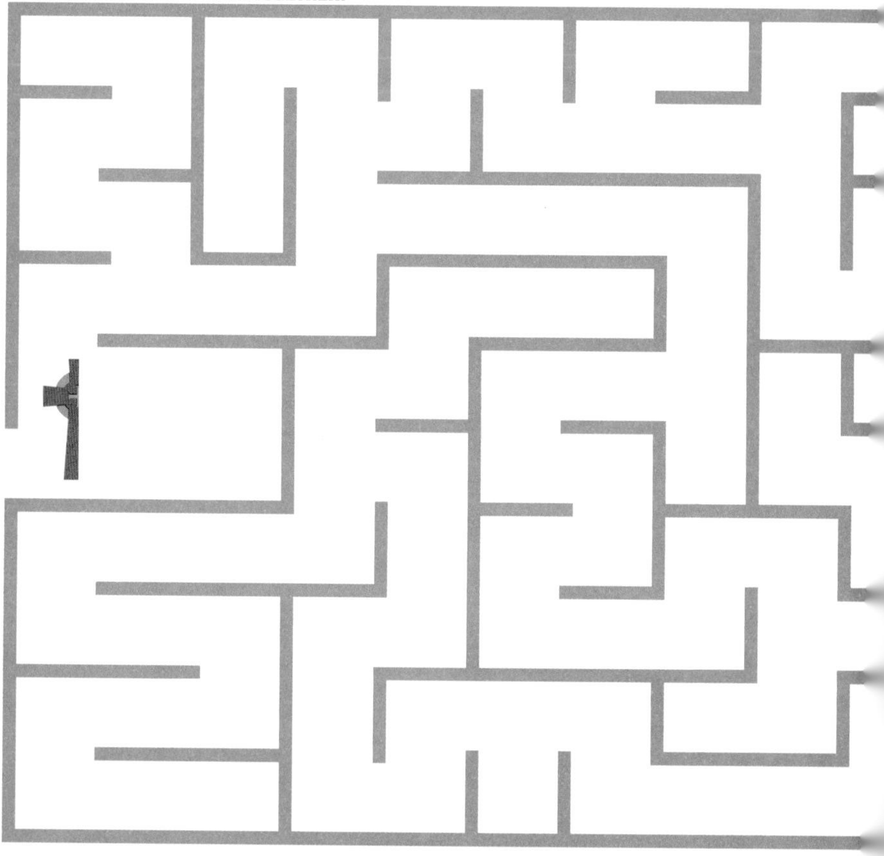

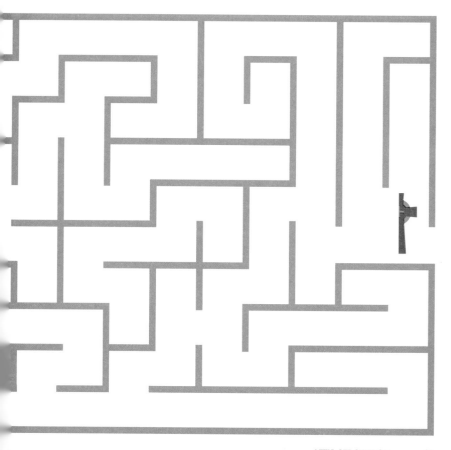

MANY IRISH PEOPLE RECOGNISE ST BRIGID'S DAY BY MAKING A BRIGID'S CROSS, BUT WHAT IS THE CROSS USUALLY MADE FROM?

A) TWINE

B) REED

C) LEATHER

GOLA
INISHBOFIN
ARRANMORE
ACHILL
VALENTIA
SKELLIGS
DURSEY
GARINISH
WHIDDY
SHERKIN

A G A R I N I S H I
B V A L E N T I A N
S K E L L I G S R I
H C J D Y R O S R S
E A C H I L L K A H
R W B P O U A L N B
K N D U R S E Y M O
I M E R T Y U I O F
N W H I D D Y O R I
D F G H J K L P E N

WHO, IN THE FOLLOWING LIST, IS NOT AN IRISH SAINT?

A) ST PATRICK

B) ST BURIANA

C) ST GERTRUDE

ANSWERS

P4-5

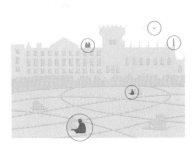

P6-7

P8-9 C) SHAMROCK ISLAND

P10-11

P12-13 A) BLACK BEER

P14-15

P16-17 B) 26
P18-19

P22-23 B) A FADED PHOTO
P24-25

P20-21

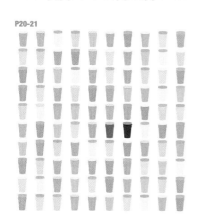

P26-27

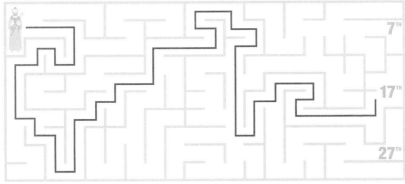

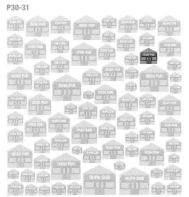

P36-37 A) SLIOTAR

P38-39

P40-41 B) 32 IN.

P42-43

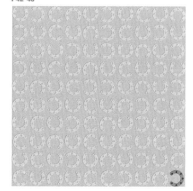

P44-45

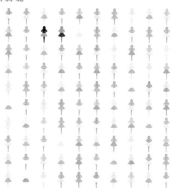

P46-47

P54-55

P54-55

P56-57 B) BOXTY

P58-59

P60-61

P62-63

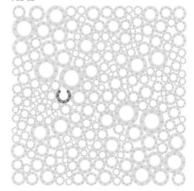

P64-65

P66-67 B) THREE WISHES

P68-69

P70-71

P72-73 C) SAMUEL BECKETT

P74-75

P76-77

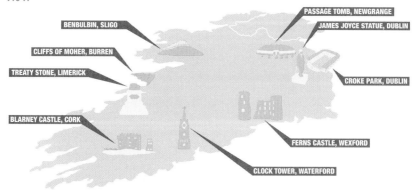

BENBULBIN, SLIGO

PASSAGE TOMB, NEWGRANGE

JAMES JOYCE STATUE, DUBLIN

CLIFFS OF MOHER, BURREN

TREATY STONE, LIMERICK

CROKE PARK, DUBLIN

BLARNEY CASTLE, CORK

FERNS CASTLE, WEXFORD

CLOCK TOWER, WATERFORD

P78-79

P80-81 C) EAT, DRINK AND BE MERRY

P82-83

P86-87 B) THE SHAMROCK

P88-89

P94-95

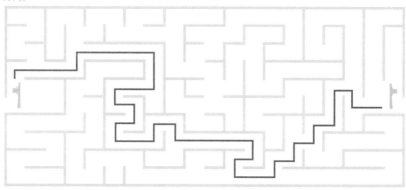

P96-97 B) REED

P98-99

P100-101 C) ST GERTRUDE

IF YOU'RE INTERESTED IN FINDING OUT MORE
ABOUT OUR BOOKS, FIND US ON FACEBOOK AT
SUMMERSDALE PUBLISHERS AND FOLLOW US ON
TWITTER AT **@SUMMERSDALE**.

WWW.SUMMERSDALE.COM

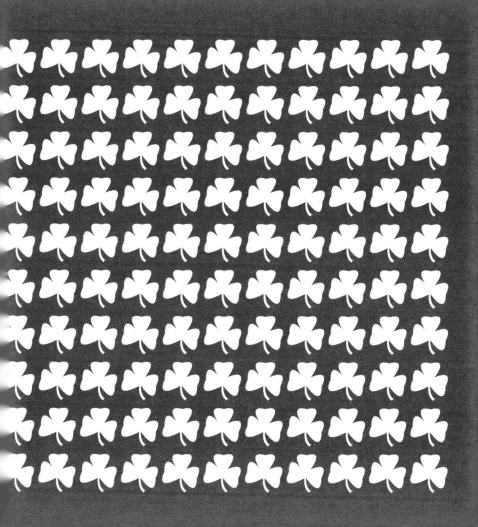

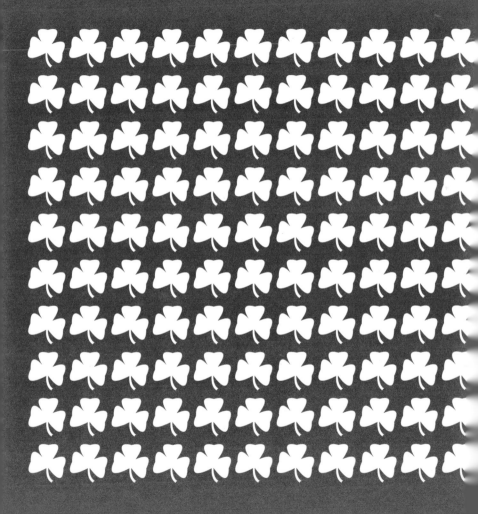